THE NEW SINCERITY

BY ALENA SMITH

★ Revised Edition

DRAMATISTS
PLAY SERVICE
INC.

THE NEW SINCERITY
Copyright © 2015, Alena Smith

All Rights Reserved

SPECIAL NOTE

Anyone receiving permission to produce THE NEW SINCERITY is required to give credit to the Author as sole and exclusive Author of the Play on the title page of all programs distributed in connection with performances of the Play and in all instances in which the title of the Play appears, including printed or digital materials for advertising, publicizing or otherwise exploiting the Play and/or a production thereof. Please see your production license for font size and typeface requirements.

Be advised that there may be additional credits required in all programs and promotional material. Such language will be listed under the "Additional Billing" section of production licenses. It is the licensee's responsibility to ensure any and all required billing is included in the requisite places, per the terms of the license.

SPECIAL NOTE ON SONGS AND RECORDINGS

Dramatists Play Service, Inc. neither holds the rights to nor grants permission to use any songs or recordings mentioned in the Play. Permission for performances of copyrighted songs, arrangements or recordings mentioned in this Play is not included in our license agreement. The permission of the copyright owner(s) must be obtained for any such use. For any songs and/or recordings mentioned in the Play, other songs, arrangements, or recordings may be substituted provided permission from the copyright owner(s) of such songs, arrangements or recordings is obtained; or songs, arrangements or recordings in the public domain may be substituted.

To Christine

The world premiere of THE NEW SINCERITY was presented by Bay Street Theater (Scott Schwartz, Artistic Director; Tracy Mitchell, Executive Director), on May 26, 2015. It was directed by Bob Balaban; the set design was by Beowulf Boritt and Alexis Distler; the lighting design was by Mike Billings; the costume design was by Maria Hooper; the sound design was by Brandon Wolcott; and the production stage manager was Jennifer Wheeler Kahn. The cast was as follows:

ROSE .... Justine Lupe
BENJAMIN .... Teddy Bergman
DJANGO .... Peter Mark Kendall
NATASHA .... Elvy Yost

CHARACTERS

ROSE, 29. An idealist.

BENJAMIN, 32. A cynic.

DJANGO, 23. An anarchist.

NATASHA, 22. An intern.

PLACE

New York, present day.

TIME

Fall to winter.
As time passes, the scene headings are projected onstage
("September"; "The Next Day").

The movement imagined in this play is similar, but not identical, to the activities known as Occupy Wall Street that took place in New York City in 2011.

"She'd mistaken us for figures of import, radicals of influence, though we knew we were not."

— Sarah Resnick
"Rumors," *n+1, Occupy! #2*

THE NEW SINCERITY

September

In the office of the literary journal Asymptote, *where a party to celebrate the release of the newest issue of the journal has just wrapped up. Minutes ago the space was full of people; now there are only two left. The music is still playing.*

Rose, a freelance writer, in dark jeans and a tank top, leans halfway out into the hallway, waving some goodbyes to the dregs of the gathering.

Benjamin, the editor, lazes on the couch in a t-shirt, nursing an expensive bottle of whiskey.

Rose dances a little, then turns off the music.

ROSE. Oh my gosh. That was a *great party*!
BENJAMIN. "Oh my gosh"? Do you really say that?
ROSE. I can't believe how many people showed up.
BENJAMIN. Yeah, I had to turn away some of the interns.
ROSE. You did not.
BENJAMIN. Yeah I did. Natasha and them. Nobody under twenty-five, I said. No little hipsters.
ROSE. Ha. Like *you'd* turn away a cute girl.
BENJAMIN. Rose, what are you implying? Remember, I'm engaged to be married.
ROSE. Oh, yes, I know. *(Beat.)* Well — congratulations.
BENJAMIN. On what?
ROSE. On the new *issue*, of the journal. I think it's really great. And it's such an honor for me, to be included.

BENJAMIN. Oh, give me a break. Your essay was the only good thing in this issue. People are raving about it.

ROSE. People are raving about my ten-thousand-word analysis of the Triangle Shirtwaist fire?

BENJAMIN. At least your piece was *serious*. Everything else was total fluff.

ROSE. I don't know if that's true …

BENJAMIN. This is a literary journal, Rose. Not a fashion magazine. Not a blog. We shouldn't even have *pictures* in our journal — it should be pure, serious writing from cover to cover. The whole intention when we started this thing was to create the next *Dissent*, the next *Harper's*, a *Partisan Review* for the post-millennium. But *unfortunately*, I wasn't born with a trust fund, so I had to partner up with a guy who carries a two-thousand-dollar handbag and thinks the best kind of article involves a line-by-line analysis of the new Rihanna.

ROSE. I don't have a problem with populism.

BENJAMIN. Gideon is not a populist, Rose. Gideon bought a townhouse in London tonight. Through an *app*. On his *phone*.

ROSE. Oh my gosh.

BENJAMIN. As long as Gideon's in charge of this journal, it will be silly and decadent. An essay about *Gossip Girl*?! I never okayed that! I'm completely anti-writing about television.

ROSE. But you wrote that thing about *The Wire*.

BENJAMIN. Rose. *The Wire* is different.

ROSE. I still haven't seen it.

BENJAMIN. Are you *kidding* me? What have you been doing with your life?!

ROSE. Well, let's see. Getting a PhD at Columbia? Writing a dissertation on romantic irony in Stendhal?

BENJAMIN. You need to go home and watch all five seasons tonight.

ROSE. Okay, I'll do that. Speaking of — I should go face the subway.

BENJAMIN. Don't leave.

ROSE. Okay.

BENJAMIN. Come sit on the couch with me.

ROSE. Oh — okay. *(She sits.)*

BENJAMIN. I'm drunk.

ROSE. I can see that.

BENJAMIN. I'm drunk and my fiancée's in Berlin. *(Beat.)*

ROSE. When does Sadie come back?

BENJAMIN. Christmas.

ROSE. Oh. That's a while.
BENJAMIN. Yeah. Fulbrights last a year.
ROSE. And when she comes back —
BENJAMIN. Well, we're on Sadie's clock here. Sadie wants to get married. Sadie wants to have a baby. And we're the same age, thirty-two, but see — for a woman, that means panic. Me, however, I have time. So, you see, we're the same age? But she's too old for me. Don't you think that's fucked up?
ROSE. That's — horrifying.
BENJAMIN. That's why she's so insecure. I hold all the cards, basically.
ROSE. But — are you in love with her?
BENJAMIN. "In love"? Jesus. Look — I'm skeptical about love. At a certain point, you just have to face it — "falling in love" is not what relationships are about.
ROSE. I don't believe that!
BENJAMIN. What do you know? You're single.
ROSE. Yeah — because I haven't found the right person yet!
BENJAMIN. Oh my god, the "right person"? You really believe in that?
ROSE. I believe I can meet someone and feel something really — deep.
BENJAMIN. Deep. Okay.
ROSE. Like — passionate. Like I can't live without this person. Like everything about me becomes *more* real and *more* alive — with them.
BENJAMIN. That sounds slightly exhausting. *(Beat.)* Anyway, that must be hard.
ROSE. What's hard?
BENJAMIN. Being single. As a woman. In New York.
ROSE. Oh, yes. Yes of course. I cry myself to sleep every night.
BENJAMIN. How old are you?
ROSE. Twenty-nine.
BENJAMIN. Okay. You have time. Just barely.
ROSE. Phew! What a relief, to hear you say that.
BENJAMIN. Well, I wouldn't get too relaxed. But you have a little bit of time.
ROSE. It must be hard for *you*. Being engaged.
BENJAMIN. How so?
ROSE. No more hookups. No more one-night-stands.
BENJAMIN. Oh, I get around.
ROSE. Benjamin — you should be careful.
BENJAMIN. What are you talking about?

ROSE. I mean I *saw* you tonight. You were flirting with all those interns.
BENJAMIN. Sadie knows I flirt with interns. She doesn't care.
ROSE. She doesn't?
BENJAMIN. Anyway — this is exactly the problem I have with the atmosphere around here. Why are people gossiping about me and Sadie? Don't we have better things to talk about? Shouldn't we be talking about — oh, I don't know — a *living wage*? Structural inequality? Even a discussion of Derrida would be preferable. That's why I like you, Rose.
ROSE. Me? I never talk about Derrida —
BENJAMIN. No. But you're serious. You're completely sincere.
ROSE. Well — gosh. Thanks. *(Beat.)* I'm sorry you had a bad time tonight.
BENJAMIN. Oh, who cares. It's all temporary. As soon as Sadie gets back from Berlin, we're moving out of this office. And we're taking Gideon's name off the masthead.
ROSE. But Gideon is your co-founder — and he pays for everything —
BENJAMIN. Yeah, but we won't need him anymore. Not when we have the apartment.
ROSE. What apartment?
BENJAMIN. Sadie's great-uncle, Herman. May he rest in peace.
ROSE. You guys are like — *inheriting* an apartment?
BENJAMIN. Yup. Soon as Sadie gets back from Berlin, and we make this shit legal, it's ours. Herman said so in his will. Man, his grandkids were pissed — but Sadie's his favorite, you know. Or if she wasn't the favorite before, she sure shot right up in the rankings once she wrote a whole book about how good old Herm was her hero. If only he could have lived to see the book published. But he did get a look at the galleys, before he departed. Sadie made sure of that.
ROSE. Smart.
BENJAMIN. Yeah, so, that's the plan. City Hall, then pack up our shit, move to West Tenth Street. Take all this with us. Hopefully have the new office set up by next issue.
ROSE. Wow. It's a real uprising.
BENJAMIN. More like a velvet divorce. Gideon can go off and start a rap dictionary or whatever the hell he wants. Meanwhile, we'll rebrand this journal. Again. Everything we publish will be thoughtful. Deep. Political. And serious.

ROSE. Well — I hope I can still write things for you. At that point.
BENJAMIN. Why wouldn't you? You're very serious. The whole reason I published your essay in this issue is that your writing embodies the quality I want for *Asymptote*.
ROSE. Yeah, but. I think Sadie hates me.
BENJAMIN. Hates you? That's absurd. Sadie likes everyone.
ROSE. Yeah, but Natasha said — oh, forget it.
BENJAMIN. Natasha? My intern, Natasha?
ROSE. Yeah, the intern. Never mind.
BENJAMIN. No, please — tell me what the twenty-somethings are tweeting behind my back.
ROSE. Okay, fine. It's ridiculous — but Natasha said that Sadie — is jealous. Of me.
BENJAMIN. Oh — well, yeah. She is.
ROSE. But *why*?! She's the one who got a hundred-*thousand* dollar book deal — not to mention a Fulbright! I'm barely scraping by!
BENJAMIN. Yeah, but you have something she doesn't.
ROSE. What do I have?
BENJAMIN. You're a good writer.
ROSE. You — Benjamin! That's awful!
BENJAMIN. Speaking as a man who has edited you both, it's just a fact. You're better.
ROSE. You just — you shouldn't *say things like that*. About your fiancée.
BENJAMIN. I know, right? What's this town coming to.
ROSE. And besides — I heard her book is *amazing*. Everybody who's read drafts of it says that it's great.
BENJAMIN. Yeah, well. She had help with that.
ROSE. What do you mean?
BENJAMIN. I pretty much ghost-wrote it for her.
ROSE. Stop.
BENJAMIN. It's true. Sadie can't write. She can self-promote. She can *operate*. But her actual voice is just — mediocre.
ROSE. Benjamin —
BENJAMIN. What, Rose.
ROSE. I just — I can't believe the stuff you say to me sometimes. *(An awkward pause.)* Anyway — I should say thank you.
BENJAMIN. For what?
ROSE. Come on. Everybody wants to get published in *Asymptote*. And you picked me. Thanks to you, I have, like, *instant* credibility.

BENJAMIN. You really shouldn't look at it that way. You're an incredibly talented writer. Like I said, your essay was the highlight of this issue. You make *us* look good.

ROSE. Really?

BENJAMIN. Yeah. So don't worry about Sadie, okay? And for god's sake don't worry about me. Just focus on your next piece.

ROSE. You want me to write something new?!

BENJAMIN. Of course. As of tonight, I'm making you a featured contributor.

ROSE. Seriously?! Oh my gosh! *(In excitement, she hugs Benjamin. It goes on a bit too long. She pulls away.)* Okay. I do have to go. *(Gathers her things and heads for the door.)*

BENJAMIN. Wait. Hang on.

ROSE. Yeah?

BENJAMIN. I have something for you.

ROSE. I already took a copy of the issue —

BENJAMIN. No, no — this. *(Hands her a key.)* A key to the office.

ROSE. Really?! I get a key?!

BENJAMIN. Well, you don't have to take it. But I thought you might find it useful. Gideon has one, I have one, a few of the other writers. So you can come here and work during the day. It's a good writing space. It's very quiet.

ROSE. That's — oh, *wow*, Benjamin! Thank you!

BENJAMIN. All yours. I mean — for the next few months.

ROSE. Why? What happens then?

BENJAMIN. Well — you know. We'll be moving. As soon as Sadie gets back.

ROSE. Oh. Right.

BENJAMIN. But, till then — all yours.

ROSE. Wow — I mean — this is great. And I'll get started on that next piece!

BENJAMIN. Terrific.

ROSE. *(Pauses by the door.)* Thanks again, Benjamin. This was a wonderful night. *(Beat.)* It's always been my dream, you know — to be part of a journal like this.

BENJAMIN. A journal like what?

ROSE. A great intellectual magazine! A journal of politics, of ideas — a journal that might actually publish something *important*.

BENJAMIN. Oh. Right. Yeah. *(Beat.)*

ROSE. You're really going to sleep here?

BENJAMIN. You're really going to leave? *(Rose looks at him, hesitates, and then exits.)*

The Next Day

In the office, bright and early. Nobody has cleaned up from the party. Rose is hard at work at the desk. The door opens and Natasha enters.

NATASHA. What are you doing here?
ROSE. Oh — hey, Natasha.
NATASHA. Is Ben here? How'd you get in?
ROSE. He just left. But he gave me a key.
NATASHA. Whaaaaaaa … t?
ROSE. What part of that sentence didn't you understand?
NATASHA. Oh, I understood every word of it, Rose. I have a rich vocabulary.
ROSE. So why are you looking at me like that?
NATASHA. Because. This is so intense. This is like — spiraling.
ROSE. Natasha. Calm down. It's just a key —
NATASHA. I had no idea things were moving so fast. Can we recap?
ROSE. Recap *what?*
NATASHA. Whatever *episodes* I missed last night.
ROSE. I don't know what to tell you.
NATASHA. I love how *reticent* you are. Is that our age difference? When I'm twenty-nine will I like, hide everything?
ROSE. Probably not.
NATASHA. No, you're right. It'll be too late for me. I've been on Facebook since middle school. My digital trails are like, epic. What do I do, delete all that stuff? Impractical. No, at this point my best bet is like, obscurity through oversharing. Put out so much data that the shit I should keep secret just gets lost in the noise. Too much to sift through. Hashtag, who cares.
ROSE. I'm not even on Facebook.
NATASHA. And that's why you're like, basically my hero.
ROSE. Okay.

NATASHA. Back to this key business. Tell me everything. Go.
ROSE. What are you asking?! Benjamin gave me a key so I could come here and write. End of story.
NATASHA. So you two *didn't* hook up.
ROSE. What?! No! He's *engaged*.
NATASHA. Oh. Believe me. I know.
ROSE. What would even make you *think* that —
NATASHA. I saw the way he was looking at you last night. And now he gives you a key? This is major. This is so major I might have to double major. In media studies. And *this*.
ROSE. Nothing is going on between me and Benjamin. Okay?
NATASHA. Rose. Listen. I just want you know. I like, *fully* support your mission.
ROSE. What mission?
NATASHA. Operation Steal Benjamin. From Sadie.
ROSE. I just *told* you — I am *not* —
NATASHA. Get it girl.
ROSE. Stop it. Okay? That's inappropriate — and borderline offensive.
NATASHA. *Fuck* that bitch.
ROSE. And here we are over the border.
NATASHA. *(In a strange voice.)* "Oh, hey, look at me, I'm in Berlin, and I'm so fancy, and I treat everyone like shit, because I'm so damaged, and no, Benjamin, you can't start a *podcast* with an *intern* even though she's done our dirty work for *seven semesters*" — Oh, I can't wait for that icy bitch to come back and find out you got her man.
ROSE. That is not going to happen.
NATASHA. *(Intensely disappointed.)* No, why not?! Do it for us, Rose. Do it for the interns.
ROSE. What are you talking about?
NATASHA. We just want her *out*. Deposed. Off with her head! You could be our new queen. Your reign would be kind, and gentle, because you're nice. Sadie's so mean, she makes him mean. But you'd make him nice! Think about it — you could change the world, Rose! Starting with *him*! *(Before Rose can respond, Benjamin enters, with a bacon-egg-and-cheese. He is very hungover. Natasha, to Benjamin, sweet as pie:)* Oh, hey, Ben! How *are* you?
BENJAMIN. Nauseous. Nauseated. Whatever the fuck. *(Flops on the couch.)* Can someone clean up in here?
NATASHA. Heard you gave Rose a key.

BENJAMIN. I heard you gave Gideon a hand-job.
NATASHA. That's not germane.
BENJAMIN. Who let you in?
NATASHA. Rose did.
BENJAMIN. Rose, stop letting people in.
ROSE. She just walked in.
NATASHA. You *told* me to come by today.
BENJAMIN. Who did?
NATASHA. You did. Last night.
BENJAMIN. I said a lot of things last night.
NATASHA. Great party. Right?
BENJAMIN. I don't remember.
ROSE. It was a lot of fun.
NATASHA. Rose, your essay is *staggering*.
ROSE. You read it?
NATASHA. Started it. Love it. Ben, how great is her essay? Is she
not, like, a *genius*?
BENJAMIN. Are you cleaning up yet, Natasha?
NATASHA. I'm just saying — this girl? This girl is special. A breath
of fresh air.
ROSE. *(Modestly.)* I'm actually working on something new — I
mean, Benjamin asked me to write another piece.
NATASHA. Oh, I bet he did.
BENJAMIN. Natasha, in case you haven't noticed, I'm having a
real *Death of Marat* moment over here. So could you just hit the
mute button? There's a giant slush pile to go through, once you
pick up those cups —
NATASHA. Why do I have to clean up? You don't even pay me.
BENJAMIN. You're an intern. You get paid in social currency.
NATASHA. Right. I get paid in love.
BENJAMIN. Cups.
NATASHA. On it! Just saying, though. Team Rose.
BENJAMIN. What?
NATASHA. Nothin'. *(She walks past Rose and whispers loudly:)*
Team Rose. (She starts to clean up the detritus from the party.)
BENJAMIN. *(To Rose.)* Maybe I shouldn't have given you that key.
ROSE. No, no — I'm so glad you did! I woke up this morning and
came straight back here — 'cause listen! I know what I want to
write next!
BENJAMIN. Okay, well — save it for when I can see straight.

ROSE. Please, can't I just give you my pitch? I'm so excited about it. And I just *know* you're gonna love it. It's everything you were saying last night, that you want.
BENJAMIN. Oh, Jesus. Fine. Hit me.
ROSE. It's about the movement.
BENJAMIN. You'll have to be more specific.
ROSE. The movement — the protesters! The people in the park.
BENJAMIN. What people? What park?
ROSE. The park, Benjamin. Right outside! People are *living there*. Haven't you seen them? Ever since last week!
BENJAMIN. Do you mean homeless people?
ROSE. No, they're not homeless — well, some of them might be. But mostly — they're protesting.
BENJAMIN. Protesting what? Having homes?
ROSE. Okay — don't be an asshole.
BENJAMIN. I'm just *asking*. What are they angry about?
ROSE. I'm actually not sure.
BENJAMIN. Ha! Fascinating.
ROSE. I mean — there's a lot. It's complicated.
BENJAMIN. Isn't that what they always say.
NATASHA. That's what my Facebook says.
ROSE. Well, yeah, I guess if you're not some ideological absolutist breaking the world down into black and white, I guess that is what you'd say.
BENJAMIN. Are you calling me a fascist, Rose?
ROSE. I'm just trying to fill you in on this *park* situation, which frankly I'm a little disturbed that you don't already *know* about, given that we're just a few blocks away, and you call yourself a *journalist* —
BENJAMIN. Okay, whoa. Calm down. I know about the stupid protesters.
ROSE. Then why were you pretending you didn't?!
BENJAMIN. Because, my head hurts. And I'm fucking with you. And because *frankly* — I think it's ridiculous.
ROSE. What's ridiculous?
BENJAMIN. Crust-punk twenty-somethings squatting in a park with bongo drums and laptops making *soup* for each other and thinking they're actually sticking it to the man. It's not only absurd — it's embarassing.
NATASHA. A guy from my film class is out there. Pierre. He's pretty hardcore.

BENJAMIN. Hardcore in what way?
NATASHA. Well, his ear gauges are huge. You could stick, like, carrots in there.
BENJAMIN. See? It's people like that. Clowns. Embarrassing.
NATASHA. Embarrassing for who?
BENJAMIN. For *whom*? For those of us on the Left who happen to be serious.
ROSE. You don't think they're serious? They're sleeping out in the cold —
BENJAMIN. Please, it's not the slightest bit cold out. Let's see what happens when winter comes — not that they'll even last that long. They'll be gone in a week, max. And the only message their little rave party will have sent will be to once again prove that the left wing of this country is frivolous, unfocused, and, in short, does not have its shit together.
ROSE. But — don't you think it's possible —
BENJAMIN. Come on! This is what Sadie's book is *about* — the death of the Left. Our grandparents were the Old Left, our parents were the New Left — and those were *serious* movements. Sadie's uncle, he was a *real* activist. And so were Sadie's parents. But their revolutions ultimately failed. And then we come along, a generation of weak hipsters incapable of working for real change. It's sad.
ROSE. But these people actually *are* trying to change something.
BENJAMIN. Uh-huh. Excuse me. *(He heads to the door.)*
NATASHA. Are you going to puke?
BENJAMIN. If we keep talking about this.
ROSE. Have you even been to the park? Have you seen it for yourself?
BENJAMIN. I don't need to see it — I've seen it before! I know what protests are like, Rose — I protested the war, both wars. When was the last time a protest did anything?
ROSE. There's a different feeling at this one. I'm telling you. And it would be amazing if *Asymptote* covered it — *before* the rest of the media catches on —
NATASHA. I love it. I think it's *majestic.*
BENJAMIN. Forget it. I'm not interested. And listen — I really don't want you going down there.
ROSE. What?
BENJAMIN. You're affiliated with us now. Your name is linked to ours. If you go down there, and get involved, and god forbid get your picture in the *Post* or something, then everybody will assume

that *Asymptote* stands in support of these morons.
NATASHA. Wait — you're saying we can't *protest*?
BENJAMIN. You can do whatever you want, Natasha. You're just an intern. Rose is a featured contributor.
NATASHA. Oh, cool.
ROSE. But — you can't tell me what to do.
NATASHA. Team Rose!
ROSE. I'm excited about this movement, Benjamin. The people in the park — they're not kidding around. They're *passionate*. And if you don't want me to write about this for you, I'm just going to find somewhere else to do it.
BENJAMIN. Ha. Well-played.
ROSE. I'm not — this isn't a game.
BENJAMIN. Oh, it's always a game. *(He exits.)*
NATASHA. *(Conspiratorial.)* They're having relationship problems.
ROSE. You mean —
NATASHA. Him and Sadie. That's why he's so stressed out.
ROSE. How do you know they have problems?
NATASHA. I hacked Sadie's email.
ROSE. You *hacked* it?
NATASHA. Well, is it hacking if you found out the password and she never changes it because she's a fool?
ROSE. Natasha. That's *shockingly* unethical.
NATASHA. Her password is *password*. Okay? *That's* shocking. Anyway, it's not like it's *juicy*. Sadie has the most boring email on the planet.
ROSE. She does?
NATASHA. Oh, yeah. It's all, like, polite logistical exchanges with sociology professors. And, like, automated updates from fitness apps? And before Uncle Herman died, she would write to him every day. About *nothing*. She signs everything "Best." It's an abyss. *(Rose giggles.)* Would you be a guest on my podcast?
ROSE. Me?
NATASHA. Yes! Oh, you'd be perfect.
ROSE. What is your podcast about? Politics?
NATASHA. Kind of. It's called "What I Had for Breakfast."
ROSE. So — it's about —
NATASHA. Whatever you had for breakfast.
ROSE. Huh.
NATASHA. It's actually pretty subversive.

ROSE. Is it?
NATASHA. Yeah. 'Cause people are always like, "Oh my god, Twitter sucks, 'cause I don't care about what you had for breakfast." But then it's like — hold up. What if you do care? What if you really *do care*? *(Rose considers this.)*

October

In the office. Rose is busily taking books off the shelves, stacking them up, organizing something. There is a knock on the door.

ROSE. It's open — come in! *(The door opens and Django enters. He wears a bandana around his neck and his hair is dirty. His eyes are the kind that girls notice.)* You find the bathroom okay?
DJANGO. Oh, yeah. That was magical.
ROSE. Brushing your teeth was magical?
DJANGO. I haven't brushed my teeth in a week. That was like a spiritual awakening.
ROSE. Can't you brush your teeth anywhere by the park? At the deli or something?
DJANGO. They stopped letting us in the deli. Only place still letting us in is the health food store, and you can't take too long in there. One guy goes in and takes too long, he'll mess it up for everybody else. Solidarity. *(He hands Rose back her key, which he must have used to get into the bathroom.)* So, this place is dope. You work here?
ROSE. Kind of. It's a literary journal? I write things for them.
DJANGO. Oh. Well — that's cool. I'm not real big on the creative writing scene. My buddy though — he does poetry readings and shit.
ROSE. It's not — they don't publish poetry. It's nonfiction. Criticism?
DJANGO. Right on.
ROSE. Where did you go to school? — Or — did you — go to college?
DJANGO. Why, you gonna judge me if I didn't?
ROSE. No! — Of course not.
DJANGO. Did *you* go to college?
ROSE. Oh — yes. Columbia. Here in New York?
DJANGO. I've heard of it. *(Beat.)*

ROSE. I have like a *ton* of debt. *(Beat.)* So, um what do you do?
— I mean, when you're not in the park.
DJANGO. Oh — I'm an artist. *(Rose notices that Django has helped himself to some of the office food.)*
ROSE. Okay, cool. What kind of — what's like, your *medium?*
DJANGO. I do all kinds of stuff.
ROSE. Okay. Can you tell me about — something?
DJANGO. I built a boat out of garbage.
ROSE. Well. Okay.
DJANGO. Yup. Seaworthy vessel. Out of old Capri Suns and shit. Sailed it all the way up the Hudson.
ROSE. Oh wait — I think I read about that!
DJANGO. No — that was the other garbage boat.
ROSE. There's been more than one?
DJANGO. Yeah, these other cats made one, and they were total media-whores. Ours was more under the radar. Intentionally. *(Beat.)*
ROSE. Oh — hey, you know what? *(Pulls out a dusty old laptop.)* Nobody uses this, but it still works. You can have it.
DJANGO. Right on! This was yours?
ROSE. No — it was Benjamin's old computer, but he donated it to the office. And nobody uses it here.
DJANGO. Who's Benjamin?
ROSE. Oh — sorry. Benjamin Wolff. He's the editor. Here? At *Asymptote.*
DJANGO. He's an ass editor?
ROSE. Ha — no — *Asymptote.* This journal? — that's the name.
DJANGO. What is that — like a math thing?
ROSE. It's when a curve tries *really* hard to meet a line, but never actually gets there.
DJANGO. Okay. "Asymptote."
ROSE. I don't know — Benjamin picked it. Ugh, Benjamin — I'm so sick of him.
DJANGO. Why?
ROSE. Because. He told me I wasn't *allowed* to go to the park. As if he controls me. Can you believe that?
DJANGO. That's fucked up.
ROSE. Right?!
DJANGO. Sounds like he's on a real power trip.
ROSE. Oh, he is. He is.

DJANGO. Well — maybe he'll change, though. Gotta give people room to change.

ROSE. Oh — yeah … Maybe. Gosh. *(Beat. She returns her attention to the books.)* Anyway — so we have all these galleys. Would galleys be okay for the library, you think?

DJANGO. What's a galley?

ROSE. Oh, it's like — the final draft, kind of? The publisher sends it to the author and a few critics, before the actual publication.

DJANGO. Okay. Like a bootleg.

ROSE. Um — yeah. Kind of. See — the cover looks weird — but it's still a book.

DJANGO. Hey, if it's books, we'll take 'em. We're not picky.

ROSE. Cool — well, don't take that one.

DJANGO. Why not?

ROSE. That's Sadie's book.

DJANGO. Who's Sadie?

ROSE. Oh — sorry! Jeez, why do I keep acting like you know these people? I'm just so used to everyone knowing them — they're like celebrities around here.

DJANGO. Who are?

ROSE. Sadie. And Benjamin. Sadie is Benjamin's girlfriend. Actually — fiancée.

DJANGO. Okay. So why can't we take this?

ROSE. Oh — I guess — I just think — you wouldn't want it.

DJANGO. Why? What's it about?

ROSE. It's about — politics.

DJANGO. Politics? That sounds good.

ROSE. Yeah, no, but — *the death of the Left.*

DJANGO. The what?

ROSE. Okay, so, Sadie's great-uncle was a communist.

DJANGO. Dope.

ROSE. Yeah, he was blacklisted and stuff. And then her parents were hippies, Weather Underground-types, civil rights demonstrators, you know.

DJANGO. Awesome.

ROSE. Yeah, but so Sadie, she looks at her family, and then she looks at herself, and she's like, why don't I fight for anything? Why am I so apathetic? And actually, she's not just talking about herself. She's talking about her generation. Meaning, us. All of us. She's basically saying that the days of bare-knuckled activism are over, and that they failed,

and nowadays, people our age, we just sort of sit here doing nothing, not working for change or justice or anything, just basically being social climbers and shopping at Crate and Barrel, because we don't believe in causes greater than ourselves anymore. Or because we don't care. Or we don't know *how* to care. Or something.
DJANGO. *(Coughs.)* That's what this book says?
ROSE. In a nutshell.
DJANGO. Well — shit, man. Fuck that! *(Hands the book back to Rose.)* I mean I'm all for different perspectives. But that one could be kind of a downer I think — for a kid who just wants a good read after getting his ass kicked by cops.
ROSE. That's what I was trying to say.
DJANGO. What about sci-fi? Do you have any sci-fi?
ROSE. *(Staring at Sadie's book.)* This is so fucked up.
DJANGO. What about like — Dean Koontz?
ROSE. Seriously — I mean — think about this. Sadie's getting all this praise, not to mention *money*, for making this big bleak prognosis about our generation — and here you are, literally *outside* her door, proving she's just not paying attention! It's infuriating!
DJANGO. What is?
ROSE. *Sadie!*
DJANGO. Who's Sadie again?
ROSE. The one who wrote this *book*! Benjamin's — whatever. Future *wife*.
DJANGO. Okay. *(Beat.)* So you have a crush on this guy.
ROSE. What? What guy?!
DJANGO. This ass editor.
ROSE. *Who* — Benjamin?!
DJANGO. Yeah. I'm pretty intuitive.
ROSE. I do *not* have a "crush" on Benjamin. In fact, I'm disgusted with him.
DJANGO. Why's that?
ROSE. Because. Like I was *saying*, he basically *ordered* me never to go to the park. Like some kind of *dictator* —
DJANGO. Yeah, you want to fuck him.
ROSE. Um — okay. You're — this is making me uncomfortable.
DJANGO. Can I tell you something?
ROSE. I guess —
DJANGO. I like your mouth.
ROSE. My — huh?

DJANGO. Did that catch you off-guard? It's just a thing I'm doing. It's a practice.
ROSE. Practicing — what?
DJANGO. Saying things like that. What I feel. What I see. Just saying them. I like your mouth. I like it a lot.
ROSE. Whoa. That's — okay.
DJANGO. Would you be excited about kissing me?
ROSE. Huh?
DJANGO. I would be excited about kissing you. That was one of the first things I thought about. When I saw you.
ROSE. Um — oh my gosh.
DJANGO. What was your experience of that?
ROSE. Excuse me?
DJANGO. This morning. In the park. When we met.
ROSE. Oh! — Um …
DJANGO. 'Cause I felt like we locked eyes. As soon as we saw each other — I felt like something, you know. Went down between us.
ROSE. You mean — by the dumpster?
DJANGO. So you know what I'm talking about.
ROSE. But — you were with that girl.
DJANGO. Which girl?
ROSE. The one you were holding hands with?
DJANGO. Oh, Alison. Not a girl.
ROSE. What?
DJANGO. Gender pronoun dragon.
ROSE. Come again?
DJANGO. Alison's preferred gender pronoun is "dragon."
ROSE. Sorry — *what?*
DJANGO. So for example, you wouldn't say, "She's in the library working group with us." You would say, "*Dragon* is in the library working group with us."
ROSE. Um, okay — but what if you wanted to be like, "Alison is *her* name"?
DJANGO. Alison is *dragon's* name.
ROSE. That's a bit much, don't you think?
DJANGO. A bit much for what?
ROSE. For — functional human society?
DJANGO. Oh, so we can have genetically modified foods and robot drones that murder children remotely, but we can't be a little creative with our gender pronouns?

ROSE. Okay. That's fair.

DJANGO. Anyway, just because I was holding hands with dragon doesn't mean I couldn't be looking at you. *(Beat.)* I think you're beautiful.

ROSE. That's — whoa.

DJANGO. Are you attracted to me?

ROSE. I — you're really putting me on the spot here, Django.

DJANGO. I like how you say my name.

ROSE. I'm just — okay, so, you and — you and *dragon* aren't, like, dating?

DJANGO. "Dating"? No.

ROSE. Okay.

DJANGO. We're fucking.

ROSE. *(Pause.) Oh.*

DJANGO. Sometimes just the two of us, sometimes with others.

ROSE. Ah … ha.

DJANGO. We're just trying to set a good example.

ROSE. A good example — for *whom*?

DJANGO. The community. Hell — the world.

ROSE. Okay.

DJANGO. No — I said that wrong. It's not about setting an example. It's not about the future. It's about now. It's about us embodying the change. Making the impossible happen, for ourselves. Right? Direct action.

ROSE. Yes — yes! Hey, Django! Could I *interview* you?!

DJANGO. About what?

ROSE. About the movement! I mean, you were one of the first people there, in the park, weren't you? You were there when the whole thing started. I mean — you *started it.*

DJANGO. Hang on — is this why you've been being so nice to me? You wanted to get me on tape?

ROSE. No! — I mean, of course not. But — why not? I mean, is that not something you'd be — up for?

DJANGO. Why would I want that?

ROSE. To show — to illuminate — um, your ideas. And what's happening. And to let people know who you are! And what you're fighting for!

DJANGO. I'm not doing this so people will know who I am.

ROSE. Well, I didn't mean that —

DJANGO. And also — I'm not fighting.

ROSE. You're not?

DJANGO. I'm not a violent person, Rose. I don't like to fight. That's not what I'm here for.

ROSE. So — what are you here for?

DJANGO. What if I said I was here to get naked with you?

ROSE. Um —

DJANGO. What if I said I was here to pleasure you.

ROSE. That is — okay. This is really weird.

DJANGO. If you're not into it, tell me. But if you are … I can think of some pretty good ways we could be spending the afternoon. *(Beat.)* Kiss me. I mean — if you want.

ROSE. Um …

DJANGO. I just brushed my teeth. *(Rose laughs. She looks at him. Thinks about it. Then stops thinking. She kisses him. He kisses her back. The door opens. Natasha enters.)*

NATASHA. *(Checking out Django, then to Rose.)* Ah, whaaaaaaaa … t?

ROSE. Oh! Natasha! — This is —

DJANGO. Nobody. I'm gonna peace out. See you at the park. *(Exits.)*

ROSE. Wait! *(He's gone.)* He forgot to take the books.

NATASHA. Dude. Okay. *Dude.*

ROSE. Dude, what.

NATASHA. There should be a *statue* of you.

ROSE. What are you talking about?

NATASHA. You are a *baller*.

ROSE. He's just — an activist.

NATASHA. Okay. I felt the vibes in here.

ROSE. You did?

NATASHA. I was *galvanized.*

ROSE. I don't think you're using that word correctly.

NATASHA. Galvanize. To shock or excite someone into taking action.

ROSE. What action are you planning to take?

NATASHA. Whatever you say. You are my commander. I doubted you at first, but now I see you had a master plan. Just let me know how I can be of service to your mission.

ROSE. Natasha, there *is no mission*!

NATASHA. Got it. Operation Steal Benjamin continues.

ROSE. Even if I *were* trying to "steal" Benjamin, how exactly would me hanging out with *Django* make that happen?

NATASHA. His name is *Django*? Stop. That is so hot. Benjamin is going to have a meltdown.

ROSE. This has nothing to do with Benjamin! And besides, he doesn't even *know* —
NATASHA. He'll know. He can sense it. Any little hint of a threat just makes him *furious*. You're crafty, Rose. And I don't mean like you have a store on Etsy. *(The two women are interrupted by the door bursting open. Benjamin enters. He does indeed seem upset.)*
ROSE. Hey! —
BENJAMIN. Yeah. Hey.
ROSE. Uh — is everything okay?
BENJAMIN. No. No, it is not.
ROSE. What's wrong?!
BENJAMIN. I think you know.
ROSE. Uh — do I?
BENJAMIN. The irony is that *Sadie* had to be the one to bring this to my attention. And she's not even in New York! She's in Berlin!
ROSE. Sadie brought — what — to your attention?
BENJAMIN. Tell me you don't have a Google alert for your name.
ROSE. A what?
BENJAMIN. A Google alert!
ROSE. Benjamin, calm down!
BENJAMIN. For your *name*, Rose. Which is now all over the *internet!*
ROSE. Wait, it is?
BENJAMIN. It was on *Gawker*, for chrissake. "Rose Spencer, twenty-nine, who writes for the *politically active literary journal Asymptote*, says she and her *cohorts* believe these goings-on in the park might prove to be the defining political movement of their generation." And there's a fucking *link* to our *website*. See? Right here.
NATASHA. Oh, snap —
ROSE. That's so crazy — Benjamin, I didn't even *mention* the journal, I swear. I don't even know how they *knew* —
BENJAMIN. Of course they knew, Rose. The guy who wrote this article went to Harvard with us. Stephen — he was at the release party! And he *hates* us. He literally, like, wants to assassinate me.
NATASHA. He does.
BENJAMIN. I've been awake since six A.M. answering *phone calls* about this. Approximately seven hundred people emailed it to me. Somebody on the *Fulbright* committee emailed it to Sadie! Fucking *Gideon* called me from a fucking *yacht* off the coast of *Miami* wanting to know what the hell was going on here. We are fucked, Rose. You have fucked us.

ROSE. I really don't understand why this is such a big deal.

BENJAMIN. Okay, well I don't have time to give you a crash course in *branding* right now. But let's just say that as the editor of this magazine, it is a *big deal* to me what *Asymptote stands for.* There is a narrative here, and I need to be in control of it. And now — despite the fact that I *warned you* — you have gone ahead and changed that narrative.

ROSE. I didn't mean to.

BENJAMIN. Well, that doesn't help us, does it.

ROSE. If you're so opposed to the movement, why don't you just say so? Call up Stephen or whoever at Gawker and just say look, the article was wrong, Rose Spencer is not our spokesperson and *Asymptote* has nothing do with this movement!

BENJAMIN. Jesus Christ. Are you really this naïve?

NATASHA. Yeah that won't work.

ROSE. What do you mean? That's *mature.* That's the *adult* way of handling this situation.

BENJAMIN. We're not dealing with adults here, unfortunately. We're dealing with children. And I can't think of anything that could make the kids at Gawker laugh harder than if I called them up making some big kind of *statement* about how we don't support these drum-circles in the park. Oh, they'd have a field day with that one! Suddenly it would be all about how *conservative* we here at *Asymptote* are, how *stodgy* and *uptight.* And then they could go back to whoever else in the park and get *their* response — oh, boy. Controversy! Pageviews!

NATASHA. Clickbait.

BENJAMIN. No. We're locked into this storyline now. The storyline where we're on the front lines of a youthful rebellion against — Jesus. I don't even know what they're against!

ROSE. If you don't even know the specifics, then how can you be so sure that you *don't* agree with them?

BENJAMIN. It doesn't matter whether I agree with them or not! That's not the point! The point is that we are not trying to look like *flakes*! *(Beat.)* This was just — irresponsible. I mean, what am I supposed to tell Sadie?

ROSE. What do you mean?

BENJAMIN. Well, she's obviously concerned. Her book is about to come out. The publishers are *very* anxious about it. And of course Sadie's anxiety is — well, typical Sadie, it's off the charts. And in this case, I don't blame her! I mean, come on, Rose! She just wrote a *very serious memoir*, the entire point of which is that movements like this one are *doomed*!

ROSE. I see.

BENJAMIN. You put us in a corner.

ROSE. Right. And the corner is, if this movement turns out to be anything other than a total failure, Sadie's book might seem a little — stupid.

NATASHA. Oh, *snap.*

BENJAMIN. Jesus. I can't stand the way women pit themselves against each other.

ROSE. I'm not — doing that.

BENJAMIN. Of course you are. And she's doing it, too. It's really kind of a drag. *(Beat.)*

ROSE. What do you want me to do?

BENJAMIN. What?

ROSE. About the article. The link. Are you asking me to do something? To help?

BENJAMIN. No. There's nothing we can do. It's too late. We're in this now.

ROSE. In what?

BENJAMIN. The defining political movement of our generation, apparently.

ROSE. I just think — you should see it for yourself.

BENJAMIN. Okay. Fine. Let's go.

ROSE. Seriously?!

BENJAMIN. It's not like I have any other choice. Let's go.

NATASHA. You convinced him!

BENJAMIN. No, she didn't.

ROSE. You'll see, Benjamin, you'll see. You're going to be surprised!

BENJAMIN. *(Putting on a jacket.)* I doubt it. Natasha — we're leaving.

NATASHA. *I* don't want to go to the park.

BENJAMIN. I don't care where you go, you just can't stay here. You don't have a key.

NATASHA. Jesus, Ben, I've been an intern here for three *freaking* years —

BENJAMIN. So what. I don't trust you. *(Natasha glares at Benjamin, and then storms out. He looks back at Rose.)*

ROSE. That was harsh.

BENJAMIN. She shouldn't take it personally. I don't trust anybody. *(Benjamin exits. Rose follows him.)* Lock the door. *(Rose locks the door.)*

Later That Day

Inexplicably, Django is now in the office. How did he get in? He's sitting in lotus position, eating another snack and reading Sadie's book. The door opens and Rose enters. She sees Django and jumps.

ROSE. Django!
DJANGO. *(Looks up from the book.)* Oh, hey.
ROSE. What are you *doing* in here?
DJANGO. Reading. This shit is fascinating.
ROSE. But — how did you get *in*? I'm sure I locked the door —
DJANGO. Yeah, you did. I have a key.
ROSE. How did you get a key?!
DJANGO. I took it.
ROSE. Took it — from where?
DJANGO. From you.
ROSE. No — I have my key.
DJANGO. I took your key this morning and made a copy of it. While you were handing out mittens. By the dumpster.
ROSE. Wait, you *stole* my key?!
DJANGO. That's not stealing. Taking something and then giving it back? Not stealing, last time I checked.
ROSE. You took the key without my permission — and then you *broke in here* —
DJANGO. Nothing is broken.
ROSE. That's not the point —
DJANGO. "From each according to his ability, to each according to his need."
ROSE. Yeah, I've read Marx, okay —
DJANGO. Who?
ROSE. Karl *Marx*? The guy who *said* that?
DJANGO. Oh, I thought that was like a catchphrase from *Teenage Mutant Ninja Turtles* or something.
ROSE. You're kidding me.
DJANGO. Of course I'm kidding. You think I don't know my *Ninja Turtles*?

31

ROSE. Django — the point is — this is not cool. You can't just —
this isn't *your space*!
DJANGO. Damn girl. You sound like the cops at the park.
ROSE. I — okay, that is not the same — no. That is not analagous.
DJANGO. I just don't look at space that way. This is just *a space*.
No one was making use of it. I came in and I did make use of it.
ROSE. Great — but the people who pay *rent* for this space might
have a problem with that logic.
DJANGO. Do you pay the rent?
ROSE. Me? No —
DJANGO. Yet you're in here. You're in the space.
ROSE. Yes, because I was given — I was *invited*.
DJANGO. Who invited you?
ROSE. Benjamin! Who is down the hall right now, by the way —
and who will be walking in here any second!
DJANGO. Does he pay the rent?
ROSE. No — but he's co-editor. With Gideon.
DJANGO. So Gideon pays the rent.
ROSE. Well — no. His father does. I think.
DJANGO. And where's his father?
ROSE. I don't know. London, maybe?
DJANGO. Sounds like we're okay then.
ROSE. No, we're not — because what am I gonna tell Benjamin?!
DJANGO. Who's Benjamin again? *(The door swings open. Benjamin
enters, ebullient, exhilarated.)*
BENJAMIN. Rose! What a *day*! *(He sees Django. Rose attempts to
run interference.)*
ROSE. Hey! — Sorry, Ben, this is —
DJANGO. Django.
ROSE. He's a member of the — he's one of the activists. We met
this morning, in the park.
BENJAMIN. *(Delighted.)* Oh, *awesome*! So awesome. Good to
meet you, man! I'm Ben. *(The two guys shake hands. Rose is relieved.)*
DJANGO. Hey, bro. How's it going.
BENJAMIN. It is going *well*, my friend. Let me tell you. I am
thrilled right now. *Thrilled!*
DJANGO. Right on!
BENJAMIN. Rose just took me over to the park — God, I'm
ashamed I hadn't made it over already. I'm just blown away, man —
Fuck! I'm still wrapping my brain around it. I mean, this is the

kind of thing you *hope* will happen — the kind of thing that *used* to happen, maybe — but it *never* happens. But now it is! Happening! Right here, in our city — right down the fucking *street*! I'm just — I'm jumping out of my skin. Literally.

DJANGO. Word, bro! That's phenomenal!

BENJAMIN. For real, I've done like a total one-eighty. I just feel bad that it took me this long to catch on! How long have you been, like, involved?

ROSE. He's been there since the beginning!

BENJAMIN. No.

ROSE. He was there the first night.

BENJAMIN. *Incredible.* And how long ago was that?

DJANGO. Thirty-one days.

BENJAMIN. Amazing. That's amazing! And how did you *know* about it? I mean how did you know to show up there in the first place?

DJANGO. There was a call that went out. A few months ago.

BENJAMIN. Went out where? How did you get the information?

DJANGO. Like — anarchist websites and shit.

BENJAMIN. Ahh. Ah-*ha*. Yes.

DJANGO. I was down in Austin at the time, hopping trains —

BENJAMIN. Hopping *trains*?

DJANGO. Yeah, you know, that whole scene. My plan was to ride out into farm country, try to get a job picking beets or whatever, but then my buddy Alison —

ROSE. The dragon.

DJANGO. Yeah —

BENJAMIN. Sorry, the what?

ROSE. Never mind. Continue.

DJANGO. Well, yeah, so, me and Alison decided to hitch our way up to New York to do this thing instead.

BENJAMIN. You mean — to protest.

DJANGO. Uh — no. It's not a protest. I mean I don't see it that way.

BENJAMIN. You don't?

DJANGO. No. See, protest is like, anger. Like living in a world where things won't go your way. Being on the outside, you know? Like other people control you. This isn't a protest. It's an *action*. It's life. It's creating our own world, the way we want it to be. Now. Together. It's like, *love* — or something. *(Benjamin's phone rings. He looks at the number, silences it, and looks back at Django.)*

BENJAMIN. That is fascinating. Listen — I have to take this call —

but don't go anywhere, okay? I have to know more about this. I want to help. We have resources here, and you can help us figure out — I want to throw *Asymptote* into this thing. It's just so exciting! *(Answering his phone.)* Gideon! You're not gonna believe this — *(Benjamin exits. Rose turns to Django, lit up.)*
ROSE. Isn't this amazing?! He had a revelation!
DJANGO. *(Genuine.)* Right on, right on!
ROSE. And he didn't even care that you were in here.
DJANGO. Oh, yeah — that was good, too.
ROSE. Django, it's like — we went *through* something together. Like things will never be the same. At the park, this afternoon, I could *see* it happening — like, in his face. I could see his face *changing*. He was completely overcome. We walked all around, we talked to people, I showed him the kitchen, the library, the comfort station, the tents. He saw everything working — and he was *so* impressed. He was like — "This is completely beyond my expectations." He was like, "Rose, oh my god, Rose, I get it." And like, "*Thank you*, Rose." And —
DJANGO. And what?
ROSE. Oh — no. Nothing.
DJANGO. Come on, what?
ROSE. Well — it's just that — while we were in the park? We were — oh, gosh. *Holding hands. (Beat.)* It's bad. I shouldn't have done it.
DJANGO. Why not?
ROSE. Because! He's — engaged.
DJANGO. Whoa. "Engaged"? That's still a thing?
ROSE. Um, yeah … and anyway — I shouldn't be telling *you* this!
DJANGO. Why not?
ROSE. Because! — We just —
DJANGO. Dude, relax. I don't believe in setting up walls like that.
ROSE. Wait — what do you mean?
DJANGO. I mean — that's just weird to me. Why try and make all that friction? Why not just let things flow. I mean — it's all just energy. Right? It's moving around, and there are no borders. I mean, there don't have to be. That's the thing — it's up to *us*! We're creating this, right now, and if we go ahead and let the borders collapse, then we're free. You can love who you want to love! There's enough to go around. No one goes hungry, once the resources are freely distributed. There's *consensus*. It's hard, it takes work, but it can happen. It's not like it's *easy*, but it's possible. It's a choice I can make, and you can make. That's all life is, in the end. Choices. Actions. You get what I'm saying, right? You get it.

ROSE. I think so …

DJANGO. Hey. *(Takes her hand.)* You're cool.

ROSE. Oh. Thanks …

DJANGO. Man. I've been doing a lot of thinking today.

ROSE. Really — what have you been thinking about?

DJANGO. Mostly about how much I'd like to go down on you.

ROSE. *(Gulping.)* You're a very honest person, aren't you, Django?

DJANGO. What's the point of lying?

ROSE. I don't know. Don't you think people lie sometimes, to get what they want? Or to like, maintain control?

DJANGO. Is that what you do?

ROSE. No! I mean — other people. *(The door opens. Benjamin enters. Rose jumps away from Django.)*

BENJAMIN. Ah! You're still here. Excellent. Listen. Everything is moving very fast. I just got off the phone with Gideon, and he approves. I also talked to Carly, Philip, and Josh. We're all in. Raring to go. There will be a meeting tonight. You should come, obviously. We'll talk strategy. An idea has already been floated about a pamphlet, or like a newsletter, with our logo and stuff, but freely distributed. All about what's happening on the ground. The marches, the outreach — and the people, of course. Profiles. We should profile you! You can be our first profile.

DJANGO. Uh — no. Not me.

BENJAMIN. But you were there from the beginning. The first night.

DJANGO. That doesn't matter. I'm not a spokesperson. And you won't find any others. Or if you do, know that they are not legitimately aligned with the movement. We don't have spokespeople. We don't have leaders.

BENJAMIN. *(Taken aback.)* Oh — wow. Okay, yeah. I think I see what you mean.

DJANGO. No offense, man.

BENJAMIN. No — no, of course!

DJANGO. I think it's great that you guys want to help. There's so much to do. This is just — this is all good.

BENJAMIN. Cool — well, at least come to the meeting tonight! It'll be here, at eight. Your voice is so important —

DJANGO. Yeah, I can't though, at night.

BENJAMIN. Why not?

DJANGO. Nights are when we need to be in the park. Lots of people come through during the day just to check it out, but nights

are when we need to hold on. Tonight is the thirty-second night. Holding it down.
BENJAMIN. Right. *Right.* Wow.
DJANGO. You should come spend the night.
BENJAMIN. What?
DJANGO. Come sleep out in the park. More bodies. More warmth.
BENJAMIN. Wow. I — uh … well, I'm not there yet. But — yeah.
DJANGO. Okay, well. "From each according to his ability."
BENJAMIN. Right! So right.
DJANGO. Good meeting you, man. Sure I'll see you around.
BENJAMIN. Oh, for *sure.* Yes.
DJANGO. And Rose — will I see you out there tonight?
ROSE. Oh — yes! Yes, definitely.
DJANGO. Think about it.
ROSE. About —
DJANGO. Yeah.
ROSE. Okay. I will.
DJANGO. Cool.
ROSE. Django —
DJANGO. Yeah?
ROSE. Be safe. *(Django kisses Rose. Benjamin is startled.)*
DJANGO. Good day. *(Django exits. Benjamin stares at Rose.)*
BENJAMIN. Um — what was *that*?
ROSE. What?
BENJAMIN. He kissed you.
ROSE. Oh — yeah.
BENJAMIN. You're okay with that?
ROSE. Actually — yes. I liked it.
BENJAMIN. Christ. Seriously?
ROSE. Yeah — why not?
BENJAMIN. Well — he's kind of a mess, isn't he?
ROSE. In what sense?
BENJAMIN. I just mean — he's not dating material.
ROSE. Why not?
BENJAMIN. Does he even have a *job*?
ROSE. Well jeez, I don't know, *Mr. Moneybags.* What, you wouldn't date someone who was unemployed? That's not very progressive.
BENJAMIN. He's way too young for you.
ROSE. I'm not as old as you are.

BENJAMIN. Ouch. *(Beat.)* Off-topic for a second, can I ask you something?

ROSE. Uh — sure.

BENJAMIN. Do you think it's okay for a guy in his thirties to kind of — let himself go? I mean does it really matter? I'm saying won't some twenty-year-old intern be just as attracted to me if not more so if I have a little belly? I mean who cares right? Won't it just be like, oh, yeah, that editor guy in his thirties who kind of has a belly, whatever, he's hot?

ROSE. *(Laughing.)* Oh my gosh, Benjamin.

BENJAMIN. Oh, don't act innocent. Now that we know you're sleeping with that hobo.

ROSE. Hey now —

BENJAMIN. Is that what you're looking for in a relationship? Dirty fingernails, maybe a tin spoon?

ROSE. I already told you. I just want something real. *(Beat.)*

BENJAMIN. Rose. I owe you an apology.

ROSE. *(Caught off-guard.)* Huh?

BENJAMIN. I know, right. This is historic. *I'm* apologizing. But — seriously.

ROSE. What are you apologizing for?

BENJAMIN. For being wrong. I was wrong. You were right. This movement — it *is* important. Or it has the potential to be. And it's absolutely right that we should be getting involved.

ROSE. You mean —

BENJAMIN. I mean *Asymptote*. The journal. We should be all over this. And we will be, starting now. Truly, Rose, I can't thank you enough. I was just coming at everything with all this *cynicism* — and then it was like, poof. I woke up.

ROSE. That makes me so happy.

BENJAMIN. Yeah. Me too. *(Beat.)*

ROSE. Ben — listen. Honestly — I wasn't trying to drag you into this. But now that it's happened — I'm glad. Things are *changing* out there. They're intensifying. There are more people every day in the park. It's growing. The world is about to change — and we can help make it happen. Now. Benjamin —

BENJAMIN. Yeah?

ROSE. I just — I want to be part of this thing. With you. *(He looks at her. She looks at him.)*

November

Evening. Benjamin and Rose enter the office together, bundled up in scarves and hats. Benjamin is on the phone as they enter. Rose unwraps her scarf and removes her coat. Benjamin watches her undress. Rose knows he is watching.

BENJAMIN. *(On the phone.)* Yeah, we're back at the office. Me and Rose. What about you guys? Uh-huh. The bridge? Yeah, no, we heard people were getting arrested on the bridge, and we weren't prepared — yeah. We're back here, we're gonna regroup, then we're going back out. Yeah, we'll definitely be at the assembly tonight. Has there been any more — have you been hearing these rumors? Yeah. About the raid. Is that what — does it look like — yeah. Uh-huh. Well, we're gonna be there. Yeah — I'm okay with getting arrested tonight. What about you guys? Uh-huh. Yeah. No — tell Gideon — what? Hello? I can't hear you. No — the chanting's too loud! Okay — fuck it — let's text! I said *let's text! (Benjamin puts his phone down on a table. Rose points anxiously at the computer screen.)*
ROSE. There are like five hundred tweets about the park getting raided tonight. People are pretty sure it's going to happen. Also Philip got arrested this afternoon, and he's still in Central Booking. Plus the cops pepper-sprayed some old ladies today and they got injured. There's a march for them at nine tomorrow morning, unless the raid happens tonight, in which case, who knows. Are you really thinking of getting arrested?
BENJAMIN. Yeah. I am.
ROSE. That's huge.
BENJAMIN. Thank you. I'm terrified. But I'm ready. And I feel like it's something I need to do.
ROSE. Be warned. It's *really* not fun.
BENJAMIN. Not at all? I thought you guys, like, sang songs and stuff.
ROSE. Yeah, that was five minutes of entertainment. Out of thirty-six hours of hell.
BENJAMIN. Gotta say, I'm not psyched about the filthy toilets. Or the possibility of getting my ass kicked in there.

ROSE. The cops are the ones who might beat you up. This tweet says the raid tonight will be scary. Paramilitary.
BENJAMIN. God, I can't believe it. Two months ago no one was taking this seriously. Now they're putting on storm trooper hats and throwing people in jail. And for what? For pitching some tents in a park? *(Rose shakes her head and flops down on the couch.)*
ROSE. My feet hurt.
BENJAMIN. *(Flops down next to her.)* Activism really takes it out of you, huh? *(Rose smiles. Benjamin swings around, puts his feet up on the armrest, and is about to lay his head in Rose's lap.)* Oh — is it cool if I just — put my head here?
ROSE. *(Awkward.)* Oh! — Um … sure. *(Benjamin lies down, stretches out, gets comfortable.)*
BENJAMIN. Ahhh. Nice. *(Rose sits very stiffly with Benjamin's head in her lap.)* What a month it's been.
ROSE. Yes. Very exciting.
BENJAMIN. Three newsletters, in the can. And I thought this last one was really exceptional.
ROSE. I agree. It was great.
BENJAMIN. They're selling them on eBay, you know.
ROSE. Wait — what?
BENJAMIN. Our newsletters. They're selling copies on eBay. Like, memorabilia.
ROSE. How much are they selling for?!
BENJAMIN. I saw one listed for forty bucks. But it hasn't been that long yet. A couple years from now they could be worth hundreds.
ROSE. That's crazy. The whole point was to hand them out for free. "Information wants to be free."
BENJAMIN. You and I both know that's a complicated statement.
ROSE. Yes. Everything's … complicated. *(Beat.)*
BENJAMIN. Rose. Can I ask you something?
ROSE. Okay.
BENJAMIN. Do you think I'm going bald?
ROSE. *(Laughing.)* Okay, that is *not* what I expected you to say.
BENJAMIN. No — just look at my hair for a second. Just investigate. Are there any signs of thinning? Any patches?
ROSE. I think your hair looks great.
BENJAMIN. Really?
ROSE. Yeah.
BENJAMIN. I like your hair too. *(Beat. This moment grows between*

them. It grows and grows until it's right on the brink of turning into something bigger — but then, Natasha enters.)
NATASHA. Hey, *co-workers. (Rose immediately stands up. Benjamin sits up. They both pretend nothing was happening.)*
BENJAMIN. What's the word, Natasha?
NATASHA. I came back to get more newsletters.
BENJAMIN. We're out.
NATASHA. Seriously?!
BENJAMIN. Yup. All gone. To the lucky five hundred who got their hands on one.
NATASHA. Why don't we just print more?
BENJAMIN. *(Shrugs.)* You can't give one to everybody.
NATASHA. Why don't we put them online?
BENJAMIN. *(Looking at Rose.)* Who's in charge around here? *(Benjamin's phone rings. He looks at it, silences.)* Have to take this. *(Answering.)* Yo! *(Benjamin leaves the room. Natasha drops to her knees in a show of obeisance to Rose.)*
NATASHA. Khaleesi.
ROSE. Natasha, get up.
NATASHA. You have done well, my precious. Soon you will sit on the Iron Throne.
ROSE. Your references are all over the place.
NATASHA. I was raised on the internet. Now. Tell me you sealed the deal with Benjamin.
ROSE. This might qualify as sexual harrassment in the workplace.
NATASHA. Except that none of us are getting paid. Stay with me. Have you done it? You've had months now. Tell me you made it happen.
ROSE. No! I'm not sleeping with Benjamin, and I'm not *going* to sleep with Benjamin, unless —
NATASHA. Aha! Unless?! Un*less…*?
ROSE. *(Finally admitting that she does have some feelings for him …)* Unless — he were to tell me — that it was over with Sadie. That he was truly, like, free. And that he loved me.
NATASHA. *Loved* you?
ROSE. Yes. Is that so impossible?
NATASHA. No — I'm just trying to picture the words coming out of his mouth. *(She pictures it.)* I don't think Benjamin is capable of love.
ROSE. Well — I do.
NATASHA. Based on what?

ROSE. Honestly? I think Benjamin has kind of — woken up. He's different now. He's nicer. He listens to people — he doesn't just talk. And he's working for something — something bigger than himself. I mean, we all are. We're all part of this thing that's happening — this really *positive* thing. And I think Benjamin feels that. And I feel it too.
NATASHA. So — what? You like, *love* him? *(Beat.)*
ROSE. Yeah. I think I do.
NATASHA. Oh, Rose. This is — *destablizing*.
ROSE. I know. But I can't do *anything* until he breaks up with Sadie. If he wants to be with me, he has to do what's right. It's on *him*. And he can't be doing anything shady.
NATASHA. *(Sighing.)* But Rose. That day will never come. Benjamin will *always* be shady. *(Benjamin enters.)*
BENJAMIN. Guys! You're not gonna believe this! Huge news.
ROSE. What happened?
BENJAMIN. There's a video of a cop — reading one of our pamphlets. Somebody down at the park caught it on their phone, and it went viral, and now it's gonna be on CNN. CNN is doing a story tonight — about *us*!
NATASHA. Whaaaaaaatttt?!
ROSE. Whoa — I can't believe this …
BENJAMIN. I know, right?! As soon as this goes on the air, the whole world will know what *Asymptote* has been doing. After tonight, we'll be part of the *history* of this movement forever!
ROSE. Yeah. Shit.
BENJAMIN. You don't seem excited.
ROSE. I just think — we need to be careful.
BENJAMIN. Careful about what? This will be huge for you, Rose! Your name is all over that newsletter — you'll probably get a book deal!
ROSE. I'm not concerned about what this will do for me. I'm worried about what it could do to the movement.
BENJAMIN. It'll be good for the movement, obviously.
ROSE. I don't know about that. I think people might get upset.
BENJAMIN. What people?
ROSE. Well, what about Django?
BENJAMIN. Wait — you're still seeing that guy?
ROSE. Kind of. I mean, yes.
BENJAMIN. I can't believe you're still seeing him.
ROSE. Why not?
BENJAMIN. I don't know — he's sketchy. He has too much hair.

I don't like him. And besides, if he's your boyfriend, why isn't he here? Where's he been?

ROSE. He's *been* in the park. Living there. Day and night.

BENJAMIN. So you go there at night and you — ew. Gross. Like, in *public*?

ROSE. He has a tent.

BENJAMIN. Okay.

ROSE. Look — that's not the point! The point is, he might not like this. And neither will Alison.

BENJAMIN. Who the fuck is Alison?

ROSE. She's — dragon's — a person. Okay? Who did a lot. And if we go on the news and take *credit* for everything, it will seem like we're saying, we're the leaders. But there aren't supposed to be leaders. This is a collective effort. This isn't about *us*. *(Beat.)*

BENJAMIN. Well — I hear your concerns. I'm not sure what I can do about them at this point, but — I hear you.

ROSE. Okay. That's a start.

BENJAMIN. You're good for me, Rose. *(Beat.)* Now. Before we head out to the General Assembly, should we go over some business? What do we have for next issue?

NATASHA. Rose told me *I* could write something.

BENJAMIN. *(To Rose.)* Did you?

ROSE. I'm just investing in our community.

BENJAMIN. So what are you going to write about, Natasha?

NATASHA. Horizontality versus verticality, vis-à-vis social structures and power dynamics.

BENJAMIN. Oh. Fun.

ROSE. So we have Natasha's essay, and we have Carly's thing about student debt —

BENJAMIN. Right, Carly's thing — and Gideon's essay on public space —

ROSE. And Josh was going to write about getting arrested.

BENJAMIN. Oh, was he? I don't think he should do that.

ROSE. Why not?

BENJAMIN. Could get a little repetitive.

ROSE. Wait, have we done something about that already? I don't think we have —

BENJAMIN. No, but I'm planning to. Myself.

ROSE. Wait, you're planning to —

BENJAMIN. Write a thing. About being arrested.

ROSE. But — you haven't even been arrested.
BENJAMIN. Yeah, but I will be. Tonight.
ROSE. Okay …
BENJAMIN. Let's tell Josh he can write about that movie thing.
ROSE. What movie thing?
BENJAMIN. That action, where they took over that warehouse and screened movies all day.
NATASHA. Josh didn't even go to that.
BENJAMIN. Did you go?
NATASHA. Yeah. I was the only one there. It was literally me in an empty warehouse watching Godard. With no one. *(Looks off.)* I was like — you guys? You guys. You guys?
BENJAMIN. Well — do you want to write about it?
NATASHA. I mean, I *could* —
BENJAMIN. Well, whatever. Just tell Josh to think of something else. And I'll go ahead and write my thing.
ROSE. But what if you don't get arrested?
BENJAMIN. I will. Don't worry.
ROSE. Okay, but — what if you *do* and you just don't have anything to say about it?
BENJAMIN. That seems unlikely. I already have the basic outline of the piece in my head.
ROSE. But it hasn't even happened to you yet.
BENJAMIN. Yeah, but I know what to expect. Even, like, the fact that there will be some aspect of the experience that I totally *didn't* expect, you know? That little epiphany.
ROSE. Okay. So I'll just mark you down for one epiphany.
BENJAMIN. Hey. Are we fighting again? *(On the table, Benjamin's phone vibrates. Natasha picks it up.)*
NATASHA. Ben — you just got a text.
BENJAMIN. Why are you looking at my phone? Give me that —
NATASHA. Gideon wants to know if you're going to the airport.
ROSE. The airport? Why? Is there some kind of action at the airport?
BENJAMIN. I can't go to the airport. I'm getting arrested.
NATASHA. Why is Gideon going to the airport? *(Beat.)*
BENJAMIN. Sadie's coming back. *(Beat.)*
ROSE. *Tonight?!*
NATASHA. Tonight?!
BENJAMIN. It was a last-minute decision. She booked the flight yesterday.

ROSE. But — *why*?! She's not even done with her Fulbright …
BENJAMIN. Yeah. I know. But she can't stand being away anymore. She hates missing out on all this.
NATASHA. FOMO?
BENJAMIN. Yeah.
NATASHA. YOLO.
BENJAMIN. Natasha — go back to the park. *(Natasha, bowing, exits. On her way out, she might sing a protest song, like "The Internationale." The door slams behind her. Rose and Benjamin are alone.)*
ROSE. Why didn't you tell me she was coming back?
BENJAMIN. Like I said — it was last-minute. *(Beat.)* Look — I told her not to come. I mean — I told her, at least finish out your residency. But she insisted. She's freaking out. About her book. I mean, obviously, it's bad timing. Nobody wants to hear about the death of the Left right now. We're going through the most progressive upheaval this city has seen in decades! And, Jesus, when I tell her about *our* book contract? I don't even know. *(Beat.)* She just feels like everything's changing, you know? Like the whole city's changing. And I'm changing. And she's not here to change with me. *(Beat.)*
ROSE. So she's on a plane right now. And you're not going to meet her at the airport.
BENJAMIN. I can't. I need to be at the park. *(Beat.)* This is what I'm living for now. This movement. This action. *(Beat.)* I mean, Rose — you understand. You've been there. Sadie hasn't been there. *(Beat.)* You know what I mean.
ROSE. Honestly, Ben — I'm really not sure I do. *(Beat.)*
BENJAMIN. Shit — the G.A. starts in five minutes. I'm sorry — I need to get down there. Rose — *(Pauses.)* Just — don't be mad at me. Okay? *(Beat.)* Fuck! — jail. Should I like, bring snacks? *(Beat. Rose sighs.)*
ROSE. No. They're not going to let you keep anything. But! — You should write a phone number down. On your arm. Because they'll take your cell, and if you don't have it memorized —
BENJAMIN. Oh, great tip. What's your number?
ROSE. My number?
BENJAMIN. Yeah. Go.
ROSE. Are you sure you want to call me?
BENJAMIN. Who else would I call? *(Beat.)* I mean — is that okay with you?
ROSE. Is what okay?

BENJAMIN. You know. For you to be my phone call. *(Rose stares at him. We hear the sound of a police siren.)*

Later That Night

Much later. We might hear police sirens and/or helicopter chopping in the distance. At the park, a massive raid is in progress. Rose, alone in the office, mans the phones and computers.

ROSE. *(On the phone, shouting.)* Natasha, are you there? Just tell them you're a journalist! A *journalist*! Natasha! What?! They took away your press pass? What the fuck — they can't do that! A *blackout*? This is illegal! This is *crazy*! They're arresting everybody — yes, Benjamin got arrested! Three hours ago — he's in the tombs! Um, disorderly conduct, I think? He was attempting to protect the library. Did you hear what happened to the books? They destroyed them! I catalogued those books myself! Sanitation trucks — they're not *garbage*! They're books! *(The door of the office opens, and Django staggers in. His face is bloodied, his clothing dirty and torn. Rose sees him and gasps.)* Shit — I have to call you back. *(Hangs up.)* Django!
DJANGO. I didn't know where else to go.
ROSE. You're bleeding — what did they do to you?! Here — sit down, sit down — lemme get you some water or something —
DJANGO. Got any Band-Aids?
ROSE. Shit, let me see — those cuts look pretty bad! Should we go to the hospital?
DJANGO. Nah, we'd be there all night. Cops were kicking everyone's ass. Loading people out on stretchers.
ROSE. Those *thugs*! This is outrageous — this is like a fascist *dictatorship* or something — what the *fuck*!
DJANGO. Ugh, I'm so embarrassed.
ROSE. *Embarrassed* — why?! You were doing an honorable thing! *They're* the ones who should be ashamed of themselves! Beating up peaceful citizens — acting like they're rounding up terrorist insurgents in a fucking *war*! Did you get a look at the guy who hit you? Did you get his badge number?

DJANGO. Yeah — it wasn't a cop.
ROSE. Wait — what? So what happened? Who did this to you?
DJANGO. *(Sighs.)* It was that dude Sparrow. From the comfort station.
ROSE. *What?*
DJANGO. You know that dude? Sparrow? White dreds?
ROSE. Yeah, I know him — we sorted the mittens that one time. *Sparrow* did this to you?!
DJANGO. Yeah. Him and that other guy, Peter. You know Peter? Anarchist, face tats, works at Banana Republic?
ROSE. Maybe — I don't know. You're saying — these two guys — they beat you up?!
DJANGO. Yeah. Humiliating.
ROSE. But — Django! *Why?!*
DJANGO. Because they're hypocrites. That's why.
ROSE. Okay …
DJANGO. Or — it was just — I don't know. Growing pains.
ROSE. What does that mean?
DJANGO. You know. Change isn't easy, man. We can't expect it to be. We need to be patient with ourselves — we can't expect to dismantle society and rebuild it without a few bumps and bruises.
ROSE. Yeah, right — so what happened?
DJANGO. They beat me up because I pleasured their women.
ROSE. Their *women?*
DJANGO. Sorry. You know I don't mean it like that. I was speaking from the caveman perspective. "Their" women. That was meant to be in quotes.
ROSE. I'm — yeah. Okay. How many women are we talking about?
DJANGO. How many? I don't know! They just kept coming to my tent!
ROSE. Wow. Okay.
DJANGO. *(Surprised.)* Wait a minute — are you upset?
ROSE. Well — I'm upset about a lot of things right now, Django. So it's confusing. But — yeah, I guess — this rankles. A bit.
DJANGO. Shit, Rose — I thought we talked about this.
ROSE. No — we did. I knew we were keeping it open. I guess I just didn't realize — *how* open.
DJANGO. Well — open means open. Right?
ROSE. I suppose so. In theory.
DJANGO. Can I be honest with you?

ROSE. You're never *not* honest with me, Django. It's slightly un-nerving.

DJANGO. Thing is — I didn't even think you liked me that much.

ROSE. What gave you that impression?

DJANGO. It's the way you talk. About that editor guy.

ROSE. Benjamin?

DJANGO. Yeah. I mean come on. It's like he's a king or something. King of this office. King of New York. It's like you're afraid of him. To be honest — it's kind of a turn-off.

ROSE. Okay …

DJANGO. 'Cause that's not what I'm into. I'm into love. Not fear.

ROSE. You know, that sounds good, Django — but your approach to love seems to come with its own difficulties.

DJANGO. What do you mean, my approach?

ROSE. I guess — when it comes to love? I'm not an anarchist. *(Beat.)*

DJANGO. At least I'm not playing games.

ROSE. What game do you think I'm playing?!

DJANGO. Oh, you're all about games. You act like you hate the guy, but what you really want is to be just like him. And you're running around behind his girlfriend's back — instead of just being real about it. You don't even care about him — you just care about his power. Anyway, I'm not stupid. I don't have that kind of power. I don't *want* that kind of power. That kind of power — that's not what this move-ment is about. Don't you realize that? *(Silence.)* Anyway — I'm gonna head out.

ROSE. Right now? You're going back to the park?

DJANGO. No, I'm done with the park. I'm done with New York, as a matter of fact. I can no longer trust this community. I need to go somewhere else.

ROSE. You think you can find a city full of trustworthy people?

DJANGO. I don't know. I was thinking I might try Los Angeles. *(Beat.)* I want to make a documentary.

ROSE. Okay.

DJANGO. I haven't started it yet. But I just have this feeling — that it could change the world.

ROSE. Do you really believe that?

DJANGO. One hundred percent. One hundred percent I do. *(Beat.)*

ROSE. Well — good luck to you, Django.

DJANGO. Rose. Before I go.

ROSE. Yes?

DJANGO. In the interest of transparency — *(Beat.)* My name isn't Django.

ROSE. It's not?

DJANGO. No. It's Rutherford.

ROSE. Huh?

DJANGO. It's Rutherford. Hargrave? The Fourth. My family is rich. Like, fucked-up rich.

ROSE. Um — whoa.

DJANGO. But I want to take all my money and do something good. Like this documentary. Actually, it's funny — it was that book that convinced me I had to make this film.

ROSE. What book?

DJANGO. Sadie's book. Scared the shit out of me. I mean — she knows her history. She gets all the facts exactly right. But she's missing something.

ROSE. What?

DJANGO. Imagination, man. *(Beat. Just then, Natasha enters. She realizes that she's interrupting something.)* You could come make this movie with me. If you want.

ROSE. Sorry, Django. I mean —

DJANGO. Rutherford. No. Okay. See ya. *(Django, aka Rutherford, exits.)*

NATASHA. *(Calling after him.)* Wait! I'll go with you! *(Django is gone. Natasha turns to Rose.)* Shit. Is. Cray.

ROSE. I'll say.

NATASHA. Sadie's back. And Benjamin is in *jail.*

ROSE. I know.

NATASHA. Okay. So it's go-time.

ROSE. What?

NATASHA. We need to seize this moment. I'm calling Sadie right now. *(Takes out her cell phone.)*

ROSE. Wait — what are you doing that for?

NATASHA. Be the change, Rose. Be the change! *(Thrusts the phone into Rose's hand.)*

ROSE. Natasha — it's ringing! What are you — what do you want me to say?

NATASHA. Revolution. The New Deal. You and Benjamin. Tell her!

ROSE. No! *(Rose hands the phone back.)*

NATASHA. Fine! Then I'll tell her myself! Hello — Sadie? Yeah, hi.

ROSE. No — stop! *(Grabs the phone back again.)* Hello? Oh — Sadie — hi! No, this is Rose. Rose Spencer? Yeah — I'm calling from Natasha's phone. Um — we just wanted to let you know that — that — *(Natasha is pumping her fist.)* That Benjamin has been arrested. Yes. For disorderly conduct. He's down in Central Booking, and — he needs you. Yes. You should go to him. *(Natasha falls to the floor in abject despair.)* Okay. Yes. That's right. Oh — and Sadie? *(Pause.)* Welcome back. *(Rose hangs up. Natasha beats her fists on the ground.)*

NATASHA. You still had a chance.

ROSE. Stop.

NATASHA. Dude! He's been like, *begging* you!

ROSE. Begging me for what?!

NATASHA. To *save* him. From marrying her!

ROSE. Oh, give me a break! You know — he's so full of shit. If he doesn't want to marry her — why can't he just be honest about how he feels?

NATASHA. Well — he's not in love with her. He told me.

ROSE. He told you that?

NATASHA. Yup. I asked him. Straight up. I go, "Are you in love with her?" And he goes, "Not really. I'm skeptical about love. Falling in love is not what relationships are about."

ROSE. I can't believe he said that to you. When were you guys even having this conversation?

NATASHA. Oh — just one night. While we were like, fucking.

ROSE. *Excuse* me?!

NATASHA. Well, it wasn't like mid-*thrust* or anything.

ROSE. Natasha! *You've* been sleeping with Benjamin?!

NATASHA. Oh, yeah. Like, *perpetually.*

ROSE. Then *why* have you been trying to get me to *steal* him?!

NATASHA. Because, Rose. You were my only hope. Benjamin would never leave Sadie for *me.* He doesn't take me seriously. I'm just an intern. But you're like — his *equal.* You stand up to him. I don't even know why you *bother,* honestly — you don't need him. You could start a journal yourself. It would be like a hundred times better than *Asymptote.* Although, TBH, I kind of think the heyday of literary journals might be over. Like, *way* over. Maybe you could start a Tumblr? But — no, that's pointless. I don't know how you change the world these days. It's intriguing.

ROSE. Are you sure that's the word you want?

NATASHA. Intriguing. Arousing one's curiosity or interest. Yeah, that's the word. *(Smiles.)*
ROSE. Natasha — you're better than you think you are.
NATASHA. Aw. Thanks, Rose.
ROSE. Maybe you should quit.
NATASHA. Yeah. I was thinking that too. Especially now that Sadie's back. Why don't you start a thing, Rose? I could work for you.
ROSE. You mean a journal?
NATASHA. Yeah. Or a food truck. Or whatever. But when we start it? Let's do a soft launch.
ROSE. Huh?
NATASHA. A soft launch. That's what nobody expects. Everyone's expecting a big giant thing, like all over social media, like noisy and huge. But we'll just sneak up on them. Soft launch.
ROSE. Natasha, I promise, if I ever decide to do that — you'll be the first person I'll call.
NATASHA. Thanks, boo. *(Natasha kisses Rose and exits, leaving Rose alone.)*

December

Evening, a month later. Christmas decorations in the office, and it's snowing outside. Benjamin, looking sharp in a tuxedo, is taking books off a shelf and packing them in a box. He's listening to some music and dancing a little.

The door opens. Benjamin wheels around to see Rose enter, in a winter coat and hat. Benjamin turns the music off.

BENJAMIN. Oh — hey. *(Beat.)*
ROSE. Hey.
BENJAMIN. What are you doing here?
ROSE. I'm here to work.
BENJAMIN. Oh. Cool.
ROSE. What are *you* doing here?
BENJAMIN. I still run this place, don't I?

ROSE. I guess. You're never here.
BENJAMIN. Well — we're moving.
ROSE. Right.
BENJAMIN. Next week, actually. I'm just here packing up.
ROSE. Packing. Okay. So what's with the tux?
BENJAMIN. You like? Isn't it dapper? I personally wish I could always be dapper. What's wrong with a man looking dapper? I've decided I'm completely anti-scruff. This whole thing where you dress like you just woke up and you don't own a mirror — I reject that. I reject it completely.
ROSE. So you're wearing a tuxedo to what, do manual labor?
BENJAMIN. Oh — no, no. We have this thing tonight. At the Bowery Hotel.
ROSE. What thing.
BENJAMIN. Sadie's book party. *(Beat.)* It's like — super-fancy. Black tie.
ROSE. Okay.
BENJAMIN. I mean, it's not just the book party — it's also a fundraiser.
ROSE. A fundraiser for what?
BENJAMIN. For the next phase. Of the movement.
ROSE. You guys are having a black-tie party for the *movement?*
BENJAMIN. Yeah, I think it should be good. The guest list is huge. Oh — no, I don't mean, like, *extensive.* Like — A-list. Socialites. Jonathan Franzen.
ROSE. I guess I missed the e-vite. *(Beat.)*
BENJAMIN. Okay, look. I guess we should talk.
ROSE. Talk?
BENJAMIN. A lot of stuff has happened. I mean — fuck. I haven't seen you since — when?
ROSE. Not since you got arrested. The night of the raid.
BENJAMIN. Seriously? Not since then?
ROSE. I haven't seen you or heard from you since you left me here that night. Oh, well — other than in the *New York Times.* I did see you there.
BENJAMIN. Oh — so you saw it! I was gonna show it to you. *(He offers her a copy of the newspaper, folded to reveal the article in question.)*
ROSE. Yeah. I saw this. *(She grabs the article and scans it again, shaking her head.)*
BENJAMIN. What'd you think?

ROSE. What did I *think*? What did I think about a three-page article anointing you and Sadie as the radical young intellectuals at the forefront of this new political revolution?

BENJAMIN. Well — what do you think of the picture? Does it make me look fat?

ROSE. Are you kidding me? *That's* what you're worried about? How about the fact that the article is full of *lies*?

BENJAMIN. What lies?

ROSE. "Benjamin Wolff has been on the vanguard of this movement since day one." How about that, for starters?

BENJAMIN. That's not a lie.

ROSE. How is that not a lie?! You were not there on day one!

BENJAMIN. Okay — whoa. You're freaking out. It's a turn of phrase.

ROSE. It's *bullshit*, Benjamin. You know it! You *know what happened!*

BENJAMIN. I *do* know what happened.

ROSE. Then why did you agree to let them print *this* in the newspaper?

BENJAMIN. Print what?

ROSE. Okay — how about this — "Benjamin's *wife*, Sadie Merkin"—

BENJAMIN. We got married.

ROSE. Yeah.

BENJAMIN. Did you get the email?

ROSE. Yeah, I got the email. I'm not finished. "Sadie Merkin *fully anticipated* the stirrings of a new populism in her *memoir*, which tracks the *evolution* of *left-wing American activism* all the way to her *own generation*" — *What?!* Since *when*?! That is the exact *opposite* of what Sadie was saying in her book! *Anticipating?* — She was ruling out the fucking possibility!

BENJAMIN. The book is different now. We added an epilogue.

ROSE. Oh. An epilogue. I see. *(Beat.)* So this is how the story gets told. You and Sadie get all the credit — and people like Django, and Alison — it's like they never existed.

BENJAMIN. Oh, is that all you care about? Credit?

ROSE. What?!

BENJAMIN. I guess you're the superficial one around here.

ROSE. Oh. Right. And I guess you're the one who really cares. *(Beat.)*

BENJAMIN. See — from my perspective — I envy people like that.

ROSE. People like what?

BENJAMIN. Marginalized people.

ROSE. Did you really just say that?

BENJAMIN. Look — think about it. Here I am, running this journal, trying to cast myself as some kind of *radical.* But we all know, the only truly radical stuff that gets made, they're the ones who make it. You guys. The outsiders. *(Beat. Rose stares at Benjamin.)* I'm always telling this to Sadie, when she has one of her breakdowns. She's like, "I'll never be as successful as you. Never." And I'm like, "Well, that might be true, but you'll get something else. You'll get that *experience* of being a woman. Being underappreciated. And that's gotta be worth something. You know? From a critical perspective." *(To Rose.)* Why are you looking at me like that?
ROSE. I guess I was just imagining — what it would be like.
BENJAMIN. What?
ROSE. Being married to you. *(Beat.)*
BENJAMIN. Okay. Look — I'm sorry you couldn't be invited tonight. The thing is, unfortunately, Sadie and I had to have a conversation. *(Beat.)* Apparently — you said something? That made her — uncomfortable.
ROSE. What? What did I say?
BENJAMIN. It wasn't what you said. It was how you said it. When I got arrested, and you told her to come bail me out?
ROSE. Yes, I remember —
BENJAMIN. Well, for whatever reason, it made her suspicious.
ROSE. Of what?
BENJAMIN. That something was — you know. Going on. Between you and me. *(Beat.)*
ROSE. I —
BENJAMIN. Look, Rose — I get it. These things happen. How could they not, in an environment like this — a small little social world like the one we have here. We're a group of very sensitive people, and we bring a lot of ourselves into our work. We have to. And you know, inevitably, it gets complicated. I mean, look, again — it makes sense to me. I get it — I get the storyline here. And I understand your motivations. Sadie and I, we never intended this, obviously, but I know — we're kind of a power couple. And you were — well. You were trying to seize power. *(Beat.)* I don't hold this against you at all. Please know that. And I still think you're a really good writer. But Sadie has basically said, well — she doesn't want me working with you anymore. So — yeah. *(Beat.)*
ROSE. Well. *(Long pause.)* I better give this back then. *(Takes the key out of her pocket and lays it on the desk.)*

BENJAMIN. What's that?

ROSE. The key.

BENJAMIN. Oh — yeah, okay, whatever. We're moving out of this space next week, anyway. Heading to West Tenth Street.

ROSE. So you got the apartment.

BENJAMIN. Yup. Tied the knot, got the apartment. It all worked out.

ROSE. Well. I'm sure you'll be very happy.

BENJAMIN. Yeah. I don't know. We probably won't. *(Beat.)* In any case, Rose, it was good working with you. And I really can't thank you enough for taking me to the park that day. It was such a great day. I'll never forget it.

ROSE. Yeah. I remember that too. *(Beat.)* But you know what? I walked by the park, just now. On my way here. *(Beat.)* And it's so strange. The park — it's empty. Empty and cold. Like nothing ever happened. *(Rose looks at Benjamin. He says nothing. He brushes a speck of dirt off his tuxedo, and exits. Rose is silent for a moment. Then, she goes over to her computer, opens it, thinks, and starts to type. A sad song of revolution comes on. The lights fade.)*

End of Play

PROPERTY LIST

Expensive bottle of whiskey
Key
Laptops, including 1 old one
Bacon-egg-and-cheese bodega sandwich
ARC books
Smartphones
Moving boxes
Copy of *The New York Times*

SOUND EFFECTS

Party/pop music
Sad song of revolution
Police siren
Sounds of a police raid: sirens, helicopters, etc.

NOTES
(Use this space to make notes for your production)

NOTES

(Use this space to make notes for your production)

NOTES
(Use this space to make notes for your production)

NOTES
(Use this space to make notes for your production)

NOTES
(Use this space to make notes for your production)